EARTH GIANT TREE GIFT SERIES - BOOK 3

Banyan Tree's Gift

ROCHELLE HEVEREN

 TREE VOICE PUBLISHING

Earth Giant Tree Gift Series: Banyan Tree's Gift

TREE VOICE PUBLISHING PTY LTD
ACN. 627 784 294 ABN . 94627784294
4 Wirreanda Court Blackburn Victoria 3130 AUSTRALIA
Phone +613 9878 4600
Email: hello@treevoice.global
www.treevoice.global

First published in 2018
Copyright text © Rochelle Heveren
Copyright © Tree Voice Publishing

business.facebook.com/TreeVoiceAuthor
www.facebook.com/RochelleHeverenAuthor
Instagram: @rochelle_with_love_x

All rights reserved. No part of this publication may be reproduced in whole or in part, stored in a retrievable system, or transmitted in any form or by any means, electronic, mechanical, photocopying, recording or otherwise, without written permission of the copyright holder or publisher.

Designed by Tree Voice Publishing Pty Ltd
Printed by Ingram Spark
ISBN: 978-0-6483521-2-9 (paperback)

 A catalogue record for this book is available from the National Library of Australia

*I know with my whole being,
that when I sit and a tree connects,
that it is never just for me.*

*This little book
has BIG heart and soul.*

*My commitment to share this with you,
my friend, is promised.*

– Love Rochelle xxx

*Sitting in the heart of the magnificent
thousand-year-old Banyan tree,
I heard a voice. The Banyan spoke great wisdom.*

*I believe the Banyan spoke with the voice,
guidance and love of the Universe
to gently return me to my own space
of "nothingness".*

Praise for 'Banyan Tree's Gift'

"To Rochelle – a sister spirit. When a tree speaks one is given a gift. Sharing what we heard is our gift to others."

Colleen Baldrica
Author, *Tree Spirit Woman*

"As ancient knowledge surges up from within each of us and we slowly begin to awaken to wisdom of Unity consciousness, our hearts cry out to be heard and felt as never before. As our search for answers continues, Mother Nature reaches out her hand to guide and nurture us through this incredible time of change. Rochelle, in her book titled Banyan tree Wisdom: My Gift to You, offers a process which brings together the concepts of living from the heart and the unique workings of Mother Nature! Rochelle shares in such a beautiful and profound way her journey of healing and awakening – a story which relates to each and every one of us. Reading through each chapter, you can feel the spirit of the Banyan tree whispering her mystical secrets, enfolding you in her arms, and embracing you with unconditional love. The sacred wisdom shared by the Banyan tree not only inspires the reader to want to know more, but also offers a safe and gentle method of healing that is both unique and life changing. On each page there are magical gems which assist in the transformation of both the inner and outer world of the reader creating greater levels of happiness and success."

Dr Geraldine Teggelove, Msc
International Best Selling Author

"One of my Banyan Tree moments after being gifted this book was a new skill that I now use every day at work and particularly when I am having family relationship issues. The Banyan's gentle reminder to reflect the power of being STILL."

Christine
Shepparton Victoria

"I couldn't put this book down! I am in awe of the author's determination to pursue a life of love, compassion and honour. What an inspiring read."

Donna
Doreen Victoria

Foreword

Banyan Tree's Gift is the channelled teachings of one of Earth's great Mothers. The wise thousand-year-old Banyan brings you comfort, support and a unique way of guiding life's journey.

She'll remind you of your dreams, childlike wonder, unique beauty, gifts and the importance of surprise. She'll guide you through the challenges of expectation, judgement, feeling wash and tumbled and being full of worry. She will help open your heart and mind to untold possibilities and assist you to live your highest truth with compassion, stillness and unique balance.

Being supported with the magic of *Banyan Tree's Gift* is like resting your back on one of the many trunks and listening to her whispers of great wisdom. Allow her words to caress you with love.

This inspiring gift book is designed to unlock your own hearts wisdom. Rochelle invites you to discover the magic love and support that she experienced, sitting in the heart of the Banyan tree.

Written in Mauritius

Contents

Introduction 1

Chapter 1: Growth 7

Chapter 2: Protected 11

Chapter 3: Allowance 15

Chapter 4: Sadness 18

Chapter 5: Nothing 22

Chapter 6: Mother's Space 26

Chapter 7: Release 29

Chapter 8: Judgement 32

Chapter 9: Finding Everything 36

Chapter 10: Dreams 40

Chapter 11: My Promise 43

Introduction

Catching the same flight that I took over four years ago strips my emotions raw once again. During my original journey I felt lost, confused, broken and determined to exchange my rehearsed life for trust, forgiveness and self-love.

This time I carry my bursting heart without the pain I felt previously. Now my heart is bursting with love for my family, friends and, importantly, for myself. Gratitude has now become my daily guide. I have learned this secret of contentment, happiness and being present in my life.

I head toward Mauritius to reunite with someone very dear to me. I am returning to a time when the universe reached up through Mother Earth and held space for me in the thousand-year-old Banyan tree.

I can't wait to sit once more in her heart centre. Heart to heart, we have much to catch up on.

As my plane heads towards her, my memory returns me to the time we first met.

At that time, a brochure told me of an amazing tree somewhere in the resort. According to the brochure, this tree was considered one of the oldest and wisest Banyan trees in all of Mauritius.

My mind replays our first meeting:

I am walking along the path towards the far-north tip. The massive tree appears in view – widespread and beautiful. Many trunks reach down to the earth and create a wide canopy spanning at least twenty metres. A few smaller trees are around the same area – they must be babies born from the original longstanding tree.

I'm amazed not only by the size of this tree but also by a certain reverence that I feel in her presence. I have the same feeling looking at her as if walking into a large cathedral. Safety and protection envelop me.

I reach the tree's centre and find a perfect clearing, just over a square metre in size. Her trunks surround this central space. I sit in the clearing and rest my back against one of her many trunks. I rest on her fallen leaves, knowing that as time has passed she too has let go of many things.

I begin to notice some little treasures that hold meaning for me. To my left sits a piece of white coral. It has been here for a long time, washed up against her trunk. To the right is a tiny bird's egg, complete except for a small quarter, a crack created by a baby bird breaking free. Nearby is a small feather – half black and half white. A tiny twig sits next to where I rest my hand. I pick it up and see it has a knot on its side. It is so detailed, yet so small and fragile.

I gather my newfound gifts. As I sit, I felt the gusty winds from the ocean brush my back.

The roots that have fallen from the Banyan's branches are deeply buried in the ground beneath me. I feel at peace.

Her trunks and branches are not completely straight. I see that like a road map her life spans many paths. She has been weathered by life, but through branching out and re-rooting her many limbs, she has the strength to stand against many storms.

I am suddenly overwhelmed by a presence. It's the presence of my new friend; like a mother she cradles me in her centre. I ask what she can teach me about life.

She answers:

It is important to go with the flow, to reach out with your branches and grasp the opportunities that await you. Remember that Mother Earth will nourish you – stay rooted in her soil so that you can reach up to the heavens above. Embrace life's challenges. They are the very things that form and make you who you are. They shape you.

Be proud of who you really are. Stand in your strength and remember that whether or not you are noticed for your beauty, your own heart sits with contentment, calm and solitude. Go to this place inside yourself – it's a beautiful place. Make it your friend.

You have come into this life just as I did – as a tiny seed. You have been watered, nourished and shaped by your environment. Forgive your past and allow the future to take you on an amazing journey. I have journeyed a life that has taken many twists and turns; it is what makes me unique.

You have noticed the treasures in my keep.

The tiny bird's egg – take this as a sign of new growth. We all started as a seed, an egg – it is our beginning. You are to remember your first birth, as well as your new rebirth. Birth is fragile, like this shell, so be gentle on yourself.

The coral has been washed and tumbled by the ocean – the deep emotions of enormity. The tiny little holes in coral represent you. Emotionally you have been washed and tumbled, and the openings that remain represent all that has been taken from you.

The leaves upon which you sit represent the release of the old. The past cannot be released until growth has happened first.

The tiny piece of me, the branch with a knot in the otherwise smooth wood, gives this twig its own character and beauty. This represents the acceptance of self. Appreciate and love self as is.

Lastly, the feather symbolises balance. A feather belongs in your wings, readying you to take flight. Be all that you are meant to be.

I remain quietly within the tree, taking in her majestic beauty and her message. I am not here by chance. It is meant to be.

CHAPTER 1

Growth

Leaving my room just minutes before sunrise, I race to where I witnessed deep beauty last time I was in Mauritius. Security guards hover curiously, so I explain my love of the Banyan tree and my earnest desire to sit at her feet, against her trunks, once more.

The guards finally leave me alone and now I am resting my back in the heart of Banyan. I hear a loving whisper, "How are you feeling?" Banyan is the first to speak.

I remember that at times she knows more than I reveal myself, so I answer honestly: "I actually feel a little sadness, remembering how I felt during my last visit."

"This sadness requires your personal honour, just like laughter, fun and joy. Being human allows all emotions. Are you also happy?"

"Yes, I am. I love being here with you after so long. I am happy you have grown larger and are honoured here by the new restaurant that enjoys shade under your expansion."

"You have grown too," Banyan observes.

"Are you referring to my extra weight?" I laugh.

Banyan lovingly says, "You have grown in many ways. Yes, your body shows expansion. Is that the source of your sadness?"

I honestly reply, "I am ashamed of the weight I have gained, and I guess that makes me sad. I didn't think I cared until I arrived here, knowing when I was here four years ago I was 30kg lighter."

Like a gentle mother Banyan adds, "To be alone right now, even feeling lonely, is exactly what you need. For now, please disconnect from everyone. You cannot go back to the same place we visited last time. This time will be different. Another journey – yes. Perhaps your weighted sadness can fall like discarded leaves."

Because we are talking about a subject with which I have battled for years, Banyan has my attention. "What do I need to do?"

"At breakfast this morning, eat emotionally," Banyan offers.

I laugh out loud, "Oh, that's what got me into this big mess in the first place!"

"Before you head to the dining hall, please close your eyes. Breathe three times into your heart, then into your head, and finally your stomach. Tune into what you need physically. Your food will provide the answer."

"Thank you – I will definitely try this today."

My stomach rumbles, so I stand up. "I will come back again later."

I figure anything is worth a try. In the end, nothing else has been completely successful.

Heading into the dining hall, I sit at my table alone. I smile at first because I am reminded of the last time here, when I sat at many tables and couches – where everything was set for two.

Closing my eyes, I breathe and check in with my thoughts, emotions and honest cravings. I will make choices that can then support what I really want.

A big fluffy omelette fills me, leaving me satisfied. My breakfast is delicious.

CHAPTER 2

Protected

Later that afternoon, I take myself back to the heart of Banyan. I sit, my heart in hers, and she reminds me once more that life will always have its ups and downs. She encourages me to look at how she has grown and to see that all of her roots sent from above are now massive trunks supporting her.

The last time, she told me to live without judgement. I needed to embrace the life I had lived, as it was my journey. I started as a tiny seed just as she had. I was to be proud of the courage it took me to go within. In my journey to self, I have learned the importance of me.

I remember back to the day when a man stalked me along the motorway. I remember strutting over the resort gardens to sit at Banyan's centre. I had asked why some guys are such jerks, playing games of intimidation, forcing me to retreat within or to run away.

I had told Banyan that as a teenager, this happened a lot. I would attract weird guys who disrespected my boundaries by stalking me. I think this may have been one of my reasons for gaining weight – to avoid attracting attention. It worked – the stalking stopped while I was overweight. I'm sure on some deep, subconscious level I also felt comforted by the protective layer surrounding me.

Once, I tried to lose weight before I was emotionally ready to change, and as soon as people noticed the weight loss, I put it all back on.

Last time Banyan and I met, I had asked her what I needed to change about myself so that I wouldn't attract bad people. I didn't want to feel intimidated by "weirdos" anymore. I had asked if I needed to stand up and take control, if I needed to stare these guys in the eye and, with all of my strength, diffuse their attempts to intimidate me. I had wondered if I needed to give something up, in order to replace it with something new within.

I remember Banyan telling me that I cannot change others around me. As I stand in the light, there will always people in darkness, jealous of what I have. Banyan told me to not fear this light within: it is my essence. Instead, I need to allow it to suffuse every part of me.

Banyan reminded me that I was safe. That day, even after experiencing danger, I was consoled by a minister and escorted by a policeman – both safe people. I need to trust that when I stand in the essence of self, I am always protected. It is not my path to fear. It is time to fully release my fear, and in its place know that I am protected.

Banyan reminded me about the holy man in the temple who blessed me with red paint, giving me protection and abundance.

Last time I met Banyan, I learned that I needed to release the fear around my marriage with Michael. When I was able to do this and replace fear with unconditional love, I opened to a new part of myself that was able to receive.

Banyan saw that if I wanted something too badly, I instinctively blocked it energetically. She encouraged me to allow the flow of what was.

Banyan also remembers this, and asks me now:

"How is everything with your husband Michael?"

"When I returned back home, it was rocky at

first. I found my whole life had gone through a big shake-up. However, I managed to stay connected to my newly-opened heart and to trust that I was finally strong enough not to fear. You assured me of my safety. Thank you so much for holding space for me, and for teaching me unconditional love."

I sit in the heart of Banyan and look around this space. She is beautiful. As always, I feel her love and guidance in my heart. She seeded something so very special, all those years ago. It was a privilege for which I was deeply grateful, and it is with this gratitude that I have returned to sit with her physically once more.

I am in no hurry to leave the heart of Banyan. I only have a few days in Mauritius this time.

CHAPTER 3

Allowance

Memories continue to flood through my mind about my last trip to Mauritius. Banyan had such a huge impact on my life. For the first time I found myself able to exist with an open heart.

Nothing has changed since I last visited – life has just continued. There may be a different view every so often, but life has a way of simply being. Back then she reminded me that there is magic in allowing myself to love every moment of my life just as it is. I do not need to constantly create something different, a diversion or a distraction. Banyan told me that without control, once I found myself, each day would be a gift. There are treasures all around; I just needed to look in the right place.

Banyan was referring to the hidden bottles that the resort hid each day. These bottles contained gift vouchers for a massage, golf lesson or a small bottle of their local rum. I found these gifts when the time was right and each was a surprise that was simply meant to be.

Another day I spoke to Banyan and asked her what I needed to know about life itself. I remember and treasure her answer.

Banyan told me that I already knew all – I just needed to learn how to still myself and listen to the wisdom already within.

Banyan told me that when I stopped looking for the answers outside of myself, I would become still; I would clearly hear the beat of my own heart.

Banyan encouraged me to listen so that I could hear the child within – take her for walks, play with her, and ask her what she would like to do. It would be a magical thing to return to looking at my life with childlike wonder.

I was taken back to a time when I thought anything was possible; to those magical nights when I would fly to faraway lands in my dreams. Banyan encouraged me to relive the mysteries that lay beyond, to dream and imagine once more, without judging myself.

The day when Banyan shared all of this with me, was deeply special. I finally finished forgiving my parents. It was on that day that the little child buried deep within emerged and became me. I was reborn to live the life I had always been meant to live.

I was grateful to the kind old lady, Banyan. I sat in silence and felt the breeze on my face. I watched the branches reaching from above, gently swaying in the wind. They reached down into the deep roots which found ground and headed into Mother Earth to be nourished, soon becoming trunks of their own. This all just happened; nature allowed it to be. Without an organic acceptance, nothing can happen as it is meant to.

Now I see Banyan's new growth – in the four years since I last saw her, she has expanded naturally.

I remember feeling finally ready to forgive my parents. At that time, I felt sad that I had ignored my inner child for so long. With childlike excitement, I was finally able to imagine how different my life might be, connecting back fully into this once-banished part of myself.

Now I am grateful that I have forgiven my parents and my inner child has grown to be the person I am today.

CHAPTER 4

Sadness

There was one very difficult day, back when I last visited Mauritius.

That day I tried calling Michael, but the call went straight to his voicemail. I was feeling abandoned. I remember questioning whether Michael was ignoring me on purpose. I wondered if this was an attempt to control me. Was this his way of letting me know that he didn't care? My mind was spinning and I was desperately trying not to ascribe meaning to everything. At my core, I felt sad. I missed my family, my life. I wondered if it had all been worth it to step out of my life as I had.

Back then, I questioned everything. I could feel myself slipping into a dark space within, even becoming paranoid. I carried a little black rock and every time something unwanted happened in my life, I would place it into the rock in my mind.

I had to make a great effort to stop over-analysing every little situation; not to place dark meanings into events that were neutral.

Banyan had shared her wisdom about this old way of living. She pointed out that it was not helping me at all. She said that by expecting something to be a certain way, I would inevitably feel disappointment when it turned out differently. Instead, she encouraged me to believe that everything happened as it did for a reason. She taught me gratitude that everything happened as it was meant to. Whilst I placed all my energy into trying to tie things down and incessantly worrying about outcomes, I would always feel drained.

I understand now that this was why I felt so low when I couldn't get in touch with Michael. At that time, it was really hard to prevent myself from placing meaning into things I knew little about.

That night I had gone to bed with deep sadness still in my heart.

At breakfast the following morning, the background music reflected my mood; it sounded like a funeral dirge. In a way I guess I felt like I was dying on the inside.

Now I imagine the devastation I would have felt if Michael had really decided that there was no space for me in his heart. At that time, I was engulfed in fear that my husband no longer loved me. Whilst I tried to divert my mind through contemplation, it didn't work.

I continue to remember those days, five years ago now.

I want to honour my marriage to Michael. At the time I first met Banyan, Michael had been in my life for 28 years. Now it has been 33 years since Michael and I first connected with each other.

Now I celebrate the fullness of my life with Michael – the laughter, the tears, the good experiences and the painful. Our marriage has not been easy. It has been like a journey of the Banyan tree – twisting and turning to accommodate life, pushing out new roots that drop to the ground over time to secure our footing once more.

We've grown our own Banyan tree. It started as a small seed of possibility and from this union sprang four more seeds – four amazing little souls. They too now follow their own paths and learn from their own lives. And, again like the Banyan, each time they reach out to form a new trunk, a new lesson is learned. It's a blessing to watch them all grow.

When I stayed in Mauritius last time, I imagined what my tree would look like without Michael's branches winding through mine.

Now I notice that I have reached out and dropped my own roots into Mother Earth. Even though I treasure the inner wovenness of Michael's and my lives, I know I can stand strong on my own.

CHAPTER 5

Nothing

One of the most difficult days in Mauritius last time came about halfway through my stay. I had disconnected energetically from everyone back home, in order to try to really deal with the patterns of my life up until then.

I had tried to avoid others as I was afraid of bursting into tears. I recall grabbing a towel from the stack beside the pool. One of the workers approached me and I began to cry. I told him that I would be OK – I was just missing my family.

He said that he was there for me, as was the whole team of staff. I was reminded that I was not alone.

I tearfully thanked him, then headed along the water's edge to find the Banyan. I told her how sad I was.

She told me that I needed to honour the sadness as I released it.

It was cold in the Banyan garden that day. The wind swept across the Indian Ocean. I was unsure how long I could stay in the cool shade by my friend. I moved to sit at a secluded pool near the Banyan, and looked out across the western ocean. The distant ocean felt like my emotions, crashing in on me. This reminded me how I had felt for the few days before I booked my original trip.

Then, to sit in the pain of the past was difficult because the past was the part of myself that I didn't choose – rather, it chose me. I knew that there are no coincidences in life, so I asked whether my old pain held another lesson about myself.

I remember moving away from the cold pool to find an umbrella to sit under, closer to the ocean. It was less windy down by the coastline; there was only a light breeze. A small reef lagoon was in front of me and I watched as fishermen cast their nets from a boat. I recall it being much quieter at that end of the resort. I was surrounded by older couples and I wished I had the courage to ask how they had kept their marriages alive over the years. Seeing their ageless enthusiasm made me decide not to wallow in my own sadness.

Once I gave my sadness the acknowledgment and respect it needed, I found I could move from wishing it would just disappear, to respectfully asking for it to leave only when it was ready to do so.

I visited the shadow parts of myself. I had come to Mauritius to mend my broken pieces. To do this I needed to disconnect from everything external. This was a profound reality, and brought with it intense fear.

One day I remember waking to the gentle, but loud, hum of the fridge just before sunrise.

I felt completely alone. I had sat in this same sadness a day earlier. However, the sorrow had given me the opportunity of going deeper into myself – I had spent a full day crying, feeling completely cracked open.

That day, after waking in the shadows, I headed to the rocks to see the sunrise. Only moments after sitting, the sun emerged, a slither of light vibrant and golden, quickly illuminated the sky with warmth. I felt the sun's glow on my face and remember being mesmerised by its beauty. I embraced the stillness.

Later that morning I received a message from a friend asking how I was.

I replied that I felt nothing; only stillness within. I told her I couldn't believe I had come all that way for nothing. I had discovered that within my shadows sat my real inner self. We were finally fully connected – my inner child and me.

It was then that Banyan told me that we all start as nothing – a small space of freedom – before we become something.

We all experience moments of nothing just before something emerges. There is the moment of absolute freedom when skydiving, just as you jump out of a plane. There is a split second when your mind is completely empty, in the "zone", in the nothingness. Rather than experiencing this nothingness as an empty space, in my many years of entering various forms of meditation, I have never experienced a stillness as deep as this.

At the beginning, there was nothing ... and in the end, there will be nothing.

CHAPTER 6

Mother's Space

When I first came to Mauritius I would sit in the centre of the Banyan tree, day after day. Even though I sometimes stood there only briefly, I craved the act of sitting in her centre as often as I could. It was always so peaceful.

I once said to Banyan that in her quiet stillness, I'd observed her growth as slow and gradual, but still magnificent. I realised that life's journey is like her growth – gentle and gradual, if we will still allow it to be – just as it is.

One day as I sat in the heart of Banyan my phone rang. It was Michael's mum, Ali.

I found myself crying as I explained the reason for the message I had left her earlier. Ali also started crying, not knowing what to say to me. She described the broken hearts I had left back home.

In my message for her I had said that a group of older Australians had arrived in Mauritius a couple of days earlier. It was nice to hear the Australian twang in their voices. One lady had reminded me of Ali. I cried when I remembered Ali hugging me in my kitchen before I left on my trip, and I was crying as I sent the message to her.

A couple of days before booking that first trip, I had told Ali that I felt so sad, and that I was struggling with Michael's inability to love me as he used to before I lost weight.

On the phone from Mauritius, I told Ali all about the Banyan tree; about how her roots had become trunks. Ali was pretty sure she'd seen one of these trees in her own travels. How perfect to receive her call whilst I sat there in the heart of Banyan! The comfort of the Banyan was like the comfort of a mother.

I remember taking some amazing art classes last time I was here. One special day the art teacher agreed to hold the class at the foot of Banyan. I hold a fond memory of heading towards the Banyan tree for our watercolour class. My teacher, the resident artist, was excited that I had developed a connection to the majestic Banyan tree.

Water-colour class was great. I managed to paint the Banyan tree, a beautiful reminder of my time there. On that day the teacher had also brought along some of his own artwork to show me. I loved it! His pieces were all very deep and thought-provoking. I told him how much I adored his work and he said that he would love for me to choose one of his works as a gift.

I refused his offer, asking to take just a copy of one instead. I selected one that strongly depicted aspects of self, a journey and the restraints of the past. He insisted I take the original.

It was perfect. I loved it. I thanked him several times for such an incredible gift. At the end of the class I walked with him towards the front entrance of the resort. We talked about his regular work as a teacher in the nearby schools – he tried to inspire the young students to find their own "inner artist". He believed that everyone had creativity and artistic ability inside. He said creativity is another expression, a language just like speaking.

I thanked him for the gift of his artwork to me.

CHAPTER 7

Release

One day when I first visited Mauritius, I decided that I wanted to release the little black rock that I had been carrying around. I saw it as symbolising all the things I needed to let go of – the things I was willing to surrender. I imagined that once I rid myself of these qualities, there would be infinite space for internal positivity.

I planned to do this with the help of Banyan. I recall heading to my friend at the end of the day, just as the sun was setting.

I had traversed a long distance – physically, mentally and emotionally – to feel able to spend time on my own without distraction. I was grateful that I had found the courage many months ago to not only look myself in the mirror, but also to strip away all that I did not recognise as me. Now I'm thankful that I recognise my own reflection.

As I held the little rock in my hand, I also held in my mind all the aspects of self. Then I released into the rock, all that no longer served me.

It was important to forgive myself for "acting strong" for so long, for pretending to be OK, in order to survive.

As I forgave myself for forgetting who I was and for allowing my heart to be closed for so long, I dug a small hole at the base of Banyan, and asked her if she would take the tiny rock and all it contained. I instantly felt complete surrender.

It was my wish and prayer to release the past, to say farewell and to forgive. I thanked myself for the lessons learned. I also felt incredible self-love.

Then I left the Banyan's centre, walked towards a nearby small pool and entered the waters. As I slowly glided through the body-temperature water, I found it difficult to determine where my body ended and the water began. I felt the water absorbing my release and forgiveness of self.

After about ten minutes, I sensed that a shift had occurred – I felt lighter. When I returned to the Banyan, I realised that I had changed; people and situations in my life would change as well.

To complete my ritual, I placed a flower as a gift where I had released my little black rock. It was done.

CHAPTER 8

Judgement

I remember the many stages of working and living beside my friend Banyan. I recall asking her one day how I could step out of my comfort zone and live without fear of judgement.

At that time, she suggested that along with letting go of my own self-judgement, would come the need to carefully discern which opinions I would allow in my life. I had to remember that my own opinion of self was a far greater measure of truth than others' opinions.

It was interesting that I gave power to strangers by trusting their opinions of me more than my own. As I realised this, I promised to always check in with myself if ever I felt judged.

I still check in in this way, asking myself what I think, how I feel, what my opinion is, and who I am empowering in my life.

During my first trip to Mauritius, I had received text messages from friends asking if I was OK and letting me know they were worried for me. I told them I was OK; I just needed to spend some time away to really get to know myself. I guess it was hard for others to understand if they had never felt the need to hide in their own lives; if they had never shut down or become so disconnected from themselves.

I was there because I became a complete stranger to myself. It was a huge process to find who I really was. It was worth the effort, as I certainly was not really living before, only surviving – just scraping by.

Maybe that's why my digestion and health had become so damaged.

I had been ignoring my sense of self for most of my life; neglecting my body and spirit whilst harbouring obsessiveness in my mind. I thought that everything was under control, yet my body and soul had been screaming to be noticed. I am now grateful that I stopped, that I realised as I looked in the mirror that I had no clue who was looking back. This gave me the opportunity to get to know *me*.

I haven't liked all that I've seen or found on this

journey to myself. I have had to reinvent some parts of myself that had been damaged or broken, and this brought much pain to my heart. Bit by bit, I had visited dead aspects of myself, and breathed life back into them.

As I began to learn to breathe again, I also began to feel. Slowly I got to know the stranger in the mirror. I wanted to be able to look into her eyes, smile and say: "Hi, I love you. I'm proud of you. What are we going to do today?"

On the journey to myself, I claimed the power, beauty and wisdom of the being I was born to be.

But there was still something else. I needed to figure out when I developed my massive fear of judgement. I remembered back to a time in kindergarten. One day I tried to share my stories of the spirit world with other kids. The following day they all poked fun at me – they thought I was crazy. This silenced me. I was sad that I could no longer show my excitement about a world that was so much a part of my life.

After kindergarten, I went to a religious school where I was taught to fear anything spiritual. I questioned my mum about the spirit world and she told me that I had a big imagination and it wasn't real. After a time, I believed her and began to fear my friends in the spirit world.

Now I understand that I learned my fear of being judged by others from having been ridiculed. When I was laughed at and became the butt of jokes at such a young age, I became terrified of what others thought. I hated to be ridiculed and mocked. That's when I became silent, vowing to never put myself in a position where others could laugh at me.

Because I was born with the ability for clear communication with the spirit world, this gave me freedom inside my mind. It was possible for me to disconnect from my body whilst unspeakable abuse was perpetrated on me. I played with my spirit-child friend, escaping what was happening. It wasn't until I was an adult and met people with similar spiritual abilities that I found myself able to talk openly about this without being mocked.

Back in Mauritius, I promised to release the hold that judgement had over me.

CHAPTER 9

Finding Everything

While in Mauritius the first time, I became good friends with the young woman working at Reception. I heard that when she was a little girl she would play along the coastline there, particularly near the tip where the old Banyan sat.

She told me that it was such a special place, especially for the locals. People used to meet at the Banyan tree for ceremonies and gatherings for a very long time before the resort was built. At the time of my first visit, the resort had only been there for about twenty years. Her own ancestors had gathered there for decades prior, and her grandmother's ashes had also been released there.

Our conversations covered topics dear to my heart. We spoke of the spirit world and the ancestors still around, guiding us from the other side of the veil. I loved hearing her stories about the old Banyan tree, about playing there as a child, and how her own ancestors were laid to rest there too.

I learned that a long time ago, the spiritual people of Mauritius would meet at the Banyan tree as a place of reverence. I too connected to the ancient wisdom held under the shade of this great tree. It was great to be with friends who understood me, and I them. A language exists when you're with old friends, one beyond words. I will always hold a place for this woman in my heart.

During the eight years that my new friend had worked at Lux, she had never before dined out with a guest. Because of our mutual connection, I was an exception. Our dinner together became an unexpected surprise – a true gift.

I was excited to learn that the Banyan was very special for Mauritian ancestors.

I knew that I was not the first to feel her wisdom – generations before me had experienced it also.

I remember asking Banyan towards the end of my first trip, whether there was anything she could tell me about the future.

Banyan told me that the future was a mystery –

it would be the surprise that awaited me. If I knew what was going to happen then the surprise would be ruined. She asked me to remember a time when I had received a gift in the past, knowing what was inside the parcel. I had had to pretend to be surprised!

Banyan assured me that pretence was a thing of the past for me. Now that I had completely found self, journeyed to the core of who I was and who I had always been, I would begin to discover the "now". I would discover excitement and surprise. I had needed to let go of so much, yet now I could reclaim even more.

I promised to remember that nothing happens by chance – and in my "nothing", I had everything.

I took the chance to listen to my own inner voice and was amazed at the outcome. I had no clue what was going to happen – yet that is precisely what made everything so worthwhile and surprising.

As my journey has continued, I have had to remember that I would never be alone. My inner child and my higher self are both guiding me.

I promised Banyan I would remember to listen, to take notice and connect with all in that heart-space in which I now resided. As I sat in my centre, I needed to remember to also sit in the centre of self.

My beauty, wisdom and power all sat in this same space within me.

CHAPTER 10

Dreams

Before I left Mauritius after my first trip, I wrote down one of my dreams. I then pondered all the things that may have prevented me from achieving this dream. I knew that the main obstacle that stood in my way was judgement; not only the worry of others judging me, but also my judgement of others.

I made a photocopy of the painting that the art teacher had given me. On the back of it, I wrote down all the things that I had given up, as well as anything that stood in the way of me achieving my dream.

I sat in the centre of Banyan and burned all the obstacles, using a whole packet of matches to ensure I destroyed every last bit. It seemed symbolic of the journey; slowly getting rid of anything that prevented my dreams. When the paper had turned to ash I buried it in the earth beneath the Banyan.

Then I read my dream aloud. *I am.*

This is what I read:

I dream that my handwritten journey will travel beyond my own discovery to inspire others, long after I have left this planet.

I placed this dream into a small pouch of fabric and asked that it be taken above so that the ancestors and the Universal Ear could hear my dream.

A friend once told me to be still and listen to the beat of my own heart – for this is the place where all my answers are held. Finally I understood the truth in these words.

I left Mauritius the first time with a prayer in my heart, and the words of the Banyan, a song in my mind. The sweet, loving words of my friend whispered in the breeze that gently caressed my face, in the earth that supported my path, and in the flowers that magically blossomed. She had planted her seed within my heart.

With unconditional love she taught me the steps to take within; to find my own beginning – my "nothing" space, the place that was once a fearful home that I avoided at all costs. She taught me that in the end it was this very silence that I craved.

In this silence I heard the voice of great wisdom; I heard my own tiny voice, a voice that had once terrified me.

Like a mother she cradled me in her centre. She made my rebirth possible.

By reaching out and expanding towards something greater while I was in the Banyan, I found the greatest gift I will ever know.

I held my own little hand, and revived all that I am.

CHAPTER 11

My Promise

When I returned back home to Melbourne after my first trip, Michael was having an evening shower. I noticed a small leaf still on the small sprig of Daphne sitting beside the Buddha in the bathroom. I joined Michael in the shower, and we intimately embraced and washed one another.

Michael softly told me how sorry he was that he'd hurt me. I also apologised. I felt deeply sorry that he was hurt by me leaving.

While Michael was drying himself with his towel, he suddenly stopped. The leaf had finally fallen! He told me that he had checked the Daphne sprig each day I was away, repeating in his head that if it was still alive, then there was still hope for our marriage.

I smiled.

The magic, the possibility! I am comforted that

all is "as it is".

I looked into the mirror and saw a little girl smiling back at me. I noticed a gleam in my eye. She saw the wonders of the world displayed on a once blank canvas, engulfed by its fragrance and satisfied by its richness. She looked at me without breaking her gaze, and I no longer needed to distract myself. Deep in her soul, I saw me. I heard her tiny voice and saw her little arms now much bigger as they wrapped around me – my own embrace. I laughed with complete happiness, with pure joy.

All these years later, my return to Mauritius is very special. I take in all of Banyan's beauty. I know that she reflects me and holds a beautiful space always for me to travel to in my dreams.

It is good to revisit what life for me was like back then and sit now in all the new ways that I live my life.

"Banyan, as I sit with you for what may be the last time, I want to express my love for you. When I had given up on myself, it was you who held a space for me. Like a mother, you encouraged me and showed me my life from a different view. Thank you."

I cross my legs and slump slightly. I am sad that

my trip is not long this time.

"My heart in your heart ... forever we are connected. Continue to share my gift," Banyan says, trying to cheer me up.

I place a small bunch of flowers at her feet that I have gathered throughout the resort. I close my eyes and hold the feeling of love.

I grasp some of her aerial roots swaying in the warm breeze.

Finally I say: "I love you."

"I be you, as you are me; bring the gift of balance back to this world." Her soft, loving voice then turns to silence.

I wait in the Banyan until it's time to go and pack my bag.

My trip home is faster than I remembered.

I touch, I feel, I look, I see, I speak, I love, I think, I consider, I walk, I breathe, I live – I am.

Also by Rochelle

Banyan Tree Wisdom: My Gift to You

Banyan Tree Wisdom: Wisdom Cards

Meeting Rosie Banyan:
Learning Forgiveness, Trust and Love

I Give You My Word: Journal

EARTH GIANT TREE GIFT SERIES
(GIFT BOOKS & AUDIO BOOKS)

Book 1: Oak Tree's Gift

Book 2: Baobab Tree's Gift

Book 3: Banyan Tree's Gift

Book 4: Rainbow Gum's Gift

ALCHEMY OILS

Banyan Tree: 'Restore Balance', 'Dream',
'Release' & 'Beauty Wisdom Power'

Oak Tree: 'Truth'

Baobab Tree 'Connection'

Banyan Tree 'Balance'

Rainbow Gum 'Joy'

www.treevoice.global

About the Author

A busy business owner, wife and mother, Rochelle thrived in the corporate and finance world in her early adult years. Then, after her fourth son, a wave of post-natal depression debilitated her, forcing her to re-visit the horrors of her sexually abusive childhood. With grit and determination she laboured against her own broken past and breathed life back into her shutdown heart, cracking open its language and capturing it in writing. She learned to trust in the universal soul path she'd stepped onto.

Each time she experienced a healing method that helped her, Rochelle became qualified in that field to then help others. She became a Bowen Therapist, Reiki and Seichem Master, Clinical Hypnotherapist using NLP methods, Journey Worker and Intuitive Healer. She also owned and ran a Day Spa and Healing Centre in North East Victoria.

Rochelle now immerses herself in connections with nature as they flow, bringing to life the lessons and messages through writing, speaking and facilitating. Her journey has led her to many parts of the globe. She has pitched to Hollywood in New York; she has hosted women's retreats in Bali; she has learned from poverty-stricken leaders in Senegal Africa; and she discovered the 'simple' life in Vanuatu.

Rochelle's message is honest, raw and authentic, and her words are greatly needed as we all navigate our next chapter here on earth.

AUTHOR, SPEAKER, ALCHEMIST, A LOVER OF NATURE AND VIBRANT LIVING

Connect with Rochelle

hello@treevoice.global

business.facebook.com/TreeVoiceAuthor

www.facebook.com/RochelleHeverenAuthor

Instagram: @rochelle_with_love_x

www.treevoice.global

www.ingramcontent.com/pod-product-compliance
Lightning Source LLC
Chambersburg PA
CBHW032051290426
44110CB00012B/1044